What Does It Mean
to Be Born Again?

Crucial Questions booklets provide a quick introduction to definitive Christian truths. This expanding collection includes titles such as:

Who Is Jesus?

Can I Trust the Bible?

Does Prayer Change Things?

Can I Know God's Will?

How Should I Live in This World?

What Does It Mean to Be Born Again?

Can I Be Sure I'm Saved?

What Is Faith?

What Can I Do with My Guilt?

What Is the Trinity?

TO BROWSE THE REST OF THE SERIES,
PLEASE VISIT: **REFORMATIONTRUST.COM/CQ**

CQ

What Does It Mean to Be Born Again?

R.C. SPROUL

ℝ *Reformation Trust*   A DIVISION OF LIGONIER MINISTRIES, ORLANDO, FL

What Does It Mean to Be Born Again?
© 2010 by R.C. Sproul

Published by Reformation Trust Publishing
a division of Ligonier Ministries
421 Ligonier Court, Sanford, FL 32771
Ligonier.org   ReformationTrust.com

Printed in China
RR Donnelley
0001018
First edition, twelfth printing

ISBN 978-1-64289-041-9 (Paperback)
ISBN 978-1-64289-069-3 (ePub)
ISBN 978-1-64289-097-6 (Kindle)

Cover design: Ligonier Creative
Interior typeset: Katherine Lloyd, The DESK

Unless otherwise noted, Scripture quotations are from the ESV® Bible (The
Holy Bible, English Standard Version®), copyright © 2001 by Crossway, a
publishing ministry of Good News Publishers. Used by permission. All rights
reserved.

Scripture quotations marked KJV are from the King James Version. Public
domain.

Library of Congress Cataloging-in-Publication Data

Sproul, R.C. (Robert Charles), 1939-2017
  What does it mean to be born again? / R.C. Sproul.
    p. cm.
  ISBN 978-1-56769-206-8
  1. Regeneration (Theology) I. Title.
  BT790.S67 2010
  234′.4--dc22

                    2010009282

Contents

Chapter One

Must I Be Born Again?

I once spoke with a gentleman who said he wanted to learn more about the Christian faith. He said he thought that he was a Christian and wanted to know more of what Christianity involved. But, he cautioned, "I don't want to be a *born-again* Christian."

When I heard that, my mind snapped back to the 1976 presidential campaign, when Jimmy Carter identified himself as a born-again Christian. About that same time, Charles Colson, who had been an adviser to President

Nixon and who became embroiled in the Watergate scandal, was converted to Christ and wrote a book titled *Born Again*, which sold millions of copies and was made into a movie by the same title. Black Panther leader Eldridge Cleaver and even Larry Flynt, the publisher of *Hustler* magazine, got into the act by announcing to the world that they had been "born again," though Flynt now calls himself an atheist.

Suddenly the term *born again*, which had been known only in a very small segment of the church, became a hot news item and started to receive national attention. It was borrowed by the secular world and applied to things outside the Christian faith. For instance, if a baseball player had a good year following a particularly bad year, it was said he was a "born-again" player.

Somewhere in all the hype, however, the true meaning of the term *born again* became obscured. As a result, much confusion exists, even within the church, as to the precise nature of the new birth. The purpose of this booklet, then, is to examine what it means, biblically and theologically, to be born again.

At the outset, I must note that the phrase "born-again Christian," in a narrow, technical sense, is a redundancy.

This is because, according to the New Testament, in order to become a Christian, one must first be born again (John 3:3–5). Therefore, if a person is born again, he or she is a Christian. So to call somebody a "born-again Christian" is like saying that such a person is a Christian Christian. The New Testament knows of no other kind of Christian.

Also, the term *born again* is a popular synonym for the theological term *regenerate*. I know of no church in the history of Christendom that has not had a doctrine of regeneration or rebirth. That is, every Christian body in Western history has had to develop some kind of concept of what it means to be reborn spiritually. This is because the concept did not originate with theologians, Bible commentators, or preachers. The very idea of spiritual rebirth has its origins in the teaching of Jesus. Since Christians identify themselves as followers of Christ, naturally they have been interested in understanding what Jesus says about this idea.

Jesus' Conversation with Nicodemus

The account of Jesus' first teaching on this subject is found in John 3. I would like to work through this passage slowly so that we can gain a solid foundation for our ensuing discussion of the new birth.

John writes, "Now there was a man of the Pharisees named Nicodemus, a ruler of the Jews. This man came to Jesus by night" (vv. 1–2a). John immediately introduces us to Nicodemus and tells us two things about his background: first, he was a Pharisee, and second, he was a ruler of the Jews. The Pharisees were a conservative religious sect known for strict obedience to the law of God. The "rulers of the Jews" were the religious authorities in Israel. The Jewish nation was under the imperial authority of Rome and was ruled by a Roman governor. However, the religious authority in Israel was vested in a group of seventy men who formed a body known as the Sanhedrin. These men were the rough equivalent of senators in the United States or cardinals in the Roman Catholic Church. When John identifies Nicodemus as a ruler of the Jews, he is clearly indicating that Nicodemus was a member of the Sanhedrin. Not all Pharisees were members of the Sanhedrin, but some members of the Sanhedrin were Pharisees. So Nicodemus was a learned and powerful man, highly trained in theology.

Nicodemus came to Jesus by night. Why did he do that? I have a suspicion that Nicodemus was slightly nervous.

He did not want to be seen publicly with Jesus, who was popular with the people but was an object of suspicion among the religious authorities. So he was discreet in his first meeting with Jesus.

However, he came with fine words: "This man came to Jesus by night and said to Him, 'Rabbi, we know that you are a teacher come from God, for no one can do these signs that you do unless God is with him'" (v. 2). It's significant that this leader of the Jews recognized Jesus as a rabbi and addressed Him with the respect that was reserved for a theologian. Nicodemus was acknowledging that Jesus was an authentic teacher of the Word of God. He then went on to declare that at least some of the Jewish leaders recognized that Jesus was a teacher sent by God, thanks to the signs He was doing. This attitude was very different from that of many in the party of the Pharisees. They did not have such a positive view of Jesus. In fact, they attributed His remarkable activities to the power of Satan (Matt. 12:22–32). But this Pharisee refused to make such an outrageous charge; rather, he came praising Jesus. He was saying, "Jesus, I recognize that You must be a teacher sent from God because no man could exercise the kind of power that You have displayed unless God was authenticating His message."

A Necessary Condition

Notice how Jesus responded. He didn't say, "I'm humbled by this honor that you've bestowed on Me, ruler of the Jews, member of the Sanhedrin; it's great to be praised by someone in such a lofty position." It's almost as if Jesus could not wait for Nicodemus to stop complimenting Him. Once Nicodemus fell silent, Jesus responded as He always did in His teaching—by cutting through the fluff and getting to the heart of the issue. He said to Nicodemus, "Truly, truly, I say to you, unless one is born again he cannot see the kingdom of God" (v. 3). In other words: "Nicodemus, stop talking about peripheral matters and personal honors. The thing I want to get across to you is this: There is something a person absolutely must do in order to see the kingdom of God."

In theology and philosophy, we enjoy making distinctions, and one distinction that is very important in these disciplines is the one between what we call a "necessary condition" and a "sufficient condition." A necessary condition is defined as something that absolutely must happen before something else can follow. For example, in order for a fire to ignite, the presence of oxygen is absolutely required. If there's no oxygen, there can be no fire. By contrast, a sufficient condition is all that is necessary for a result to occur. Oxygen is not a sufficient condition for fire. It is necessary for fire, but alone it does not guarantee the result of fire. You cannot have fire without oxygen, but you can have oxygen without having a fire. In short, a necessary condition is a *sine qua non*—that without which the desired effect will not follow.

Jesus gave a necessary condition in this conversation with Nicodemus. Anytime Jesus teaches necessary conditions, our ears should perk up, but that is especially true in this case because He articulates an absolute requirement for entrance into the kingdom of God. He said, "*Unless* one is born again, he *cannot* see the kingdom of God." That is, *unless* "A" takes place, "B" *cannot* possibly follow. Do you see why that is so important? With these words, Jesus laid out the necessary condition for coming into His kingdom. He interrupted this man who was highly trained in theology, who was a religious ruler, who was recognized and praised by his fellow citizens in Israel, and hit him right between the eyes with the truth: "You need to be born again." It's as if I were to walk into a minister's church, and while he was asking me a theological question or saying something kind to me, I said: "Hold it. You can't even see the kingdom of God because you need to be born again." It is no wonder the Pharisees were so hostile toward Jesus.

To put it as simply as I can, if you are not spiritually reborn, you are not a Christian. It is necessary to be reborn to be a Christian. No one is born a Christian. No one enters into this world already incorporated into the kingdom of God. The Pharisees thought that they were born into the kingdom of God. They reasoned: "We're the children of Abraham. We do all the right things. We have the law of Moses." But Jesus later would say to them: "You are not the children of Abraham. You are the children of those whom you serve" (see John 8:39–47).

I cannot emphasize enough how radical this pronouncement of Jesus was. It sounds radical to our ears, and it sounded even more radical to the contemporaries of Christ.

Think back to my friend who said, "R. C., I want to become a Christian, but I don't want to be a born-again Christian." Essentially, he wanted to have his cake and eat it too. In all probability, he merely meant, "I want to be a Christian, a real Christian, but I don't want to be one of those people who wears it on his sleeve and annoys others with his obnoxious methods of evangelism." That was how he was identifying a group of Christians that made him uncomfortable, a style within the Christian church that he perceived as unique to "born-again Christians."

But in the actual meaning of the language, there is only one kind of Christian. There are different styles of that one kind of Christian. Some are polite and some are rude. Some are quiet and some are vociferous. Some are conservative and some are not so conservative. But the only kind that gets into the kingdom of God is the regenerate kind, because Jesus made the new birth a necessary condition. So the first thing that I want to communicate about rebirth is that it is necessary.

Jesus' Use of Repetition

The Jews had two ways in which they used repetition for emphasis, and Jesus used them both in His conversation with Nicodemus. I explored one of these ways in my book *The Holiness of God* when I examined Isaiah 6, where the seraphim in the heavenly throne room of God are depicted singing "Holy, holy, holy" in antiphonal response. I explained the significance of this repetition of a word, a technique we see used throughout the Bible. When the Jews wanted to make something emphatic, instead of adding an exclamation point or using italics, they would simply repeat it.

When Jesus introduced His necessary condition, He did not simply say, "Unless one is born again, he cannot see the kingdom of God." Instead, He began by saying, "Truly, truly," which, in the original language, would have read, "*amēn, amēn.*" We get the English word *amen* from this Hebrew word; it is a word we often use to end our prayers, by which we say, "Truly" or "So be it." From time to time, Jesus prefaced His teaching by the repetition of the word *amen*, and this is one of those occasions. When Jesus said, "Truly, truly," it was as if He was saying, "You had better put an asterisk next to this because it is extremely important."

In my seminary classes, I used to tell my students, "Anytime you see me write something on the board, you should put a red 'X' next to it in your notes, because you can be sure that it is going to be on the examination." Jesus did something similar when He said, "Truly, truly." When He wanted to say, "Here's something that's very important," He would say, "Truly, truly."

There are thousands of ministers in the United States of

America who will stand up this Sunday morning and say that it is not necessary to be born again in order to enter the kingdom of God. If you hear someone say that, let me ask you to remember that that is not what Jesus said. When you feel conflicted about whether being born again is or is not a requirement, you will have to decide who speaks with the supreme authority for the Christian church. The Lord of the church says, with emphasis, "Truly, truly, I say to you, unless one is born again, he cannot see the kingdom of God."

There was a second way in which the Jews used repetition. In addition to repeating a word, they would repeat a particular concept in slightly different wording. When the apostle Paul was warning the Galatians not to abandon the biblical gospel, he said to them, "Even if we or an angel from heaven should preach to you a gospel contrary to the one we preached to you, let him be accursed" (Gal. 1:8). Then the apostle added, "I say again: If anyone is preaching to you a gospel contrary to the one you received, let him be accursed" (v. 9). Paul used the second form of Jewish repetition here, making the same point twice with slightly different words.

Jesus did the same. He first said, "Truly, truly, I say

to you, unless one is born again he cannot see the kingdom of God" (John 3:3). Nicodemus replied: "How can a man be born when he is old? Can he enter a second time into his mother's womb and be born?" (v. 4). Then Jesus responded, "Truly, truly, I say to you, unless one is born of water and the Spirit, he cannot enter the kingdom of God" (v. 5). The Lord's repetition of this key requirement shows how essential it is.

Here's what I deduce from the teaching of Jesus Christ: It is impossible to see the kingdom and to enter the kingdom unless one is born again. But that raises an important question: What does it mean to be "born again"? As I said before, every church has some doctrine of regeneration. Believe me, they don't all have the same doctrine. All acknowledge that regeneration or rebirth is a requirement to get into the kingdom of God, but not all agree on how that requirement is fulfilled and precisely what is involved. In the chapters that follow, we will turn our attention to discerning just what Jesus meant when He laid down this necessary condition.

Chapter Two

Regeneration
Is a Mystery

I once saw an artist on television doing a painting demonstration. As he was painting, he explained the techniques that he was using. He started off by painting some billowy clouds. Then he demonstrated the use of a different brush to shade the clouds and to add swirls. He noted that there is a difference between a picture of clouds that are stationary in the sky and clouds that are being blown by the wind. Those that are stationary almost look paralyzed—frozen on the canvas, as it were. Real clouds, the man explained, not only have moisture in them but are blown by the wind. Then he took a third brush and moved his hand in such a way as to add marks (almost lines) to the tops of the clouds. The lines were not symmetrical, but they clearly delineated the edges of the clouds. When he finished, the clouds appeared to be moving and swirling up. I could almost feel the wind in the picture, even though I could not see the wind itself.

After teaching Nicodemus about the absolute necessity of the new birth, Jesus went on to make an analogy between the wind and the secret, mysterious inward work of spiritual rebirth. In this chapter, we will focus in on this aspect of regeneration.

"The Holy Spirit Did It All"

Some years ago, I had an opportunity to talk privately for an hour with a gentleman whom I previously had met very briefly on just one occasion. The man was the evangelist Billy Graham. I had the opportunity to eat dinner with him in Asheville, North Carolina. We discussed several things on that occasion, but in the middle of our discussion, after we each had shared our conversion experiences,

Billy related to me what had happened to him as a young man when he came under the influence of the preaching of Mordecai Ham, a speaker doing a series of services in Charlotte, North Carolina. Billy had mentioned this episode of his life many times in sermons and books, but to hear it from him personally after all the years was a very humbling experience for me.

What came across in his story was that he seemed as excited about it as if it had happened that very day. He was still filled with a passion that had been kindled years earlier in that moment when he met Christ. He described all the things that he went through as he was drawn to Mr. Ham's services and listened night after night until he finally was irresistibly drawn to Christ. In the end, Billy looked at me and said, "The Holy Spirit did it all." He was talking about being born of the Spirit.

My wife says something similar with regard to her conversion. Vesta and I had dated for about five years, and we were planning to be married. Suddenly, in my freshman year of college, I was converted, and I was told very early in my pilgrimage of faith that as a Christian I was not permitted to marry a woman who was not a believer. But Vesta was the woman I wanted to marry and to whom I was already engaged. This became a fierce conflict for me at that point in my life.

For her part, Vesta was struggling with this strange behavior that had taken over her fiancé. I had not previously possessed any serious religious persuasion, but now Christianity had turned my life upside down. She didn't know whether I was losing my mind.

A few months after my conversion, Vesta made plans to come visit me. On the day that she was to arrive, I skipped classes, stayed in my room, and locked the door. I got on the floor beside my bed and prayed like I never had prayed before. I said, "God, I don't know what the eternal decrees are, but if You have one that doesn't fit my preference here, please change it." I wrestled with God for hours on that occasion. Finally, I made a commitment that if Vesta did not become a Christian that weekend, I would break up with her. I put it on the line.

When Vesta arrived, we went to a meeting of the Christian organization in which I was involved. I didn't tell Vesta what I had prayed and what I had decided. I didn't say, "Look, if you don't come to Christ this weekend, I want the ring back." I said nothing about it. So she came to our meeting, and quite apart from me, she met Christ in that meeting. When she came out of the meeting, she was so excited. She was like Archimedes leaping out of the bathtub screaming, "Eureka, I have found it!" She knew what every Christian knows—the joy of her redemption.

But when she went to bed, all night long she kept waking up and pinching herself, saying: "Is it still there? Do I still have it?" Then she would check her internal feelings and say, "Yes, it's still there." So she'd roll over and go back to sleep.

The next morning when we got together, she told me about her experience of the night. Then she made this comment to me, which I'll never forget: "Now I know who the Holy Spirit is." I had been trying to explain to her what had happened to me, but it was like trying to explain a rainbow to a blind man. Only when Vesta believed and trusted Christ did she come to a personal understanding of the identity and the character of God the Holy Spirit. She had previously heard of the Spirit. She had been reared in regular church attendance. She had heard the benediction pronounced in the name of the Father, the Son, and the Spirit. But it had been all ceremony to her; there was no personal substance or application in her religious background. But when she was converted, she came to know the Spirit.

The difficulty I experienced in explaining my conversion to Vesta is not uncommon. One of the most difficult things in the world to articulate is what it means to have a spiritual experience that changes your life. This is because the new birth is a mystery. And if it is a mystery to those of us who have experienced it, it is an impenetrable mystery at the most fundamental level for those who have not experienced it—even for skilled theologians like Nicodemus.

Regeneration Is Mysterious

Nicodemus' confusion was evident in his conversation with Jesus. After Jesus told him, "Unless one is born again he cannot see the kingdom of God" (John 3:3), Nicodemus looked at Jesus and said, "How can a man be born when he is old? Can he enter a second time into his mother's womb and be born?" (v. 4). In other words, he said, "Jesus, what are you talking about?" I believe that is one of the most crass comments anyone ever made to Jesus. Nicodemus clearly missed Jesus' meaning.

Jesus was talking about regeneration. Notice the prefix *re*, which means "again." The word *generate* literally means "to become" or "to happen." Thus, Jesus was saying that something must "happen again." However, He did not have a physical rebirth in mind, but a spiritual rebirth. The new birth is a real birth, but it is a birth of another kind.

In response to Nicodemus' questions, Jesus began to explain this mystery. He said, "That which is born of the flesh is flesh, and that which is born of the Spirit is spirit" (v. 6). Jesus was making an obvious point, an elementary point, but one that needed repeating for Nicodemus' ears. After all, where most professional theologians go astray is not at some technical point of theology, but at a foundational point, an elementary point, a point they should have mastered. In fact, later on in this conversation, Jesus mildly rebuked Nicodemus, saying, "Are you the teacher of Israel and yet you do not understand these things?" (v. 10). It is as if Jesus was saying: "Shame on you. You should know these things. I'm not making these things up. These are the ABCs of biblical religion."

The new birth is necessary because that which is born of the flesh is flesh—and you can't get spirit out of flesh. If you want to grow an oak tree, you've got to plant an acorn, not a strawberry. The flesh yields only flesh. But that which is born of the Spirit is spirit. So Jesus was talking to Nicodemus about spiritual rebirth, not the mere repetition of a biological process. This is something far more mysterious.

Having established that He was speaking about spiritual things, Jesus added, "Do not marvel that I said to you, 'You must be born again'" (v. 7). If there is any injunction uttered by Jesus of Nazareth that people have ignored, it's that one. People still get astonished, uptight, and nervous when someone suggests that it's necessary to be reborn. But Jesus said: "Don't be amazed by that. Don't marvel at that."

Then Jesus began to answer Nicodemus' question about "how." But in addressing the mystery, Jesus actually deepened it. He said: "The wind blows where it wishes, and you hear its sound, but you do not know where it comes from or where it goes. So it is with everyone who is born of the Spirit" (v. 8). There's a marvelous play on words here. The Greek word *pneuma* can be translated as "spirit," "breath," or "wind." Thus, when Jesus said, "You have to be born of the Spirit, and it's like the wind," He was saying that the *pneuma* is like the *pneuma*. The same kind of wordplay appears in John's account of an event that occurred in the upper room, when Jesus breathed on His disciples and said to them, "Receive the Holy Spirit" (John 20:22). The word translated as both "breathed" and "Spirit" is *pneuma*. Jesus "pneumatized" (breathed on) His disciples and then said, "Receive the Holy *Pneuma*."

Jesus effectively said: "Nicodemus, do you want to know how regeneration takes place? The *Pneuma*, the Spirit, blows where it wills. It's like the wind, blowing wherever it wishes. You cannot see it, but you can see the effects of it. That's the way the *Pneuma* is." In other words, the Holy Spirit's work of rebirth is mysterious.

Regeneration Is Invisible

On a very basic level, the work of the Spirit is mysterious because there is a great deal of mystery associated with the Holy Spirit Himself. One of the greatest works ever written in the history of the church on the person and work of the Holy Spirit was by Abraham Kuyper, a theologian who also served as prime minister of the Netherlands. In the introduction to his classic book *The Work of the Holy Spirit*, Kuyper writes:

Christ can be seen and heard; once men's hands could even handle the Word of Life. But the Holy

21

Spirit is entirely different. Of Him nothing appears in visible form; He never steps out from the intangible void. Hovering, undefined, incomprehensible, He remains a mystery. He is as the wind! We hear its sound, but can not tell whence it cometh and whither it goeth. Eye can not see Him, ear can not hear Him, much less the hand handle Him. There are, indeed, symbolic signs and appearances: a dove, tongues of fire, the sound of a rushing, mighty wind, a breathing from the holy lips of Jesus, a laying on of hands, a speaking with foreign tongues. But of all this nothing remains; nothing lingers behind, not even the trace of a footprint.[1]

In short, the Spirit is mysterious because He is invisible, and His work of regeneration is mysterious for the same reason. No one can see what God is doing in someone else's soul. That's why we're warned in the Scriptures that while man looks on the outward appearances, God looks on the heart (1 Sam. 16:7). Regeneration is a spiritual reality that

---

1 Abraham Kuyper, *The Work of the Holy Spirit* (London: Funk & Wagnalls, 1900), 6.

takes place inside a person, transforming that person, but it is invisible, just like the wind.

While regeneration is invisible, we need to take note that Jesus said we can see the effects of it, just as we see, hear, and feel the effects of the wind. Where do we look for the tangible manifestations of rebirth? We see it in the fruits of a changed life.

All of us struggle as we evaluate our Christian lives. We can see changes in our lives for the good, but we also see the things we don't want to see—the things we don't want anybody to see. So as we're analyzing the states of our souls, we need to ask not where we were when we were born again or even how it happened. Rather, we need to ask whether there is any evidence of a change in the inner direction of our disposition, our attitude toward the things of God.

Unregenerate people are, at best, indifferent to the things of God. More often, they are openly hostile toward Him. Oh, some may seem to be seeking God, but Romans 3:11 tells us that is not the case. The unregenerate person never seeks God; he is a fugitive from God. Jesus came to seek and to save the lost (Luke 19:10). He is the Seeker; we are the ones who are running. The unregenerate are seeking happiness, peace of mind, relief from guilt, a meaningful life, and a host of other things that we know only God can give them. But they are not seeking God. They are seeking the benefits of God. Natural man's sin is precisely this: He wants the benefits of God without God Himself.

But when the Holy Spirit does His mysterious work of regeneration, the first thing that changes in a person is the disposition of his or her soul. Now he cares for the things of God and desires to seek God. Now there is an affection for God that was not there before. It is far from perfect, but it is real. Its origins and its power remain mysterious. But the reality is that the person's heart is beating for God, whereas it never did before. This is the undeniable effect of the blowing of the *Pneuma* through the soul.

Chapter Three

Regeneration Is the Beginning

Regeneration is the first step in the total experience of redemption that God takes us through. When people say that they're born again, they often think that their rebirth is the same thing as their new life. After all, the New Testament says that the person who is in Christ is a new creature: "Therefore, if anyone is in Christ, he is a new creation. The old has passed away; behold, the new has come" (2 Cor. 5:17). The fact that someone is a new person, a new creation, means that he has a new life, but his new life is not the same thing as his new birth. Rather, his new life is the result of his new birth, in the same way that each day of his life is the result of his physical birth. Each of us has a birthday each year, but we are not born each year. Birth happens once, and it indicates the beginning of one's existence as a person in this world. So we make a distinction between the beginning and the life that flows out of that beginning, both in terms of natural (physical) birth and with regard to supernatural (spiritual) birth, which is what we're describing by the term *regeneration.*

When I became a Christian, I found I strongly related to 2 Corinthians 5:17. I was one of those people who had a very sudden and dramatic conversion. During the first two months of my Christian experience, I was on an emotional roller-coaster ride with respect to my spiritual life. I went from spiritual ecstasy to profound spiritual depression. It was very like my experience with the game of golf. I don't know how many thousands of times I've said to my wife: "I've found it. I've got the secret. I'm never going to hit another bad golf shot. I'm never going to have another bad round." That lasts for about two days, then I'm searching all over again, because success at golf goes as fast as it comes. That's the way my Christian experience was the first two months. I went from spiritual highs to a profound sense of the absence of God, when I would fall back into old sin patterns.

This persisted until I sought help from a minister who gave me this wise counsel: "Remember that your rebirth is just the beginning. The New Testament says that although you may be an adult in every other respect (maturity, sophistication, formal education), if your Christian experience is a new thing to you, then spiritually speaking, you're a baby. You are in your infancy."

Consider the emotional patterns of infants. Have you ever noticed how changeable they are? A baby may be crying lustily, but if you say, "Goo, goo, goo" and call his attention to something else, suddenly he's giggling. But ten seconds later, he can be crying again. A child's emotions are like that until he gets to a point where the highs and lows are less extreme. Likewise, in spiritual growth, we tend to follow a generally upward trend in which our ups and downs, over time, become less severe. As we grow in maturity, we settle into a more consistent pattern of spiritual behavior.

But rebirth is merely the beginning point of this process that goes on until we're glorified in heaven. The struggle continues from the day of rebirth until that day in heaven when we reach the fullness of maturity in Christ.

I get annoyed when I hear well-intentioned preachers, in an attempt to convince people of the riches of the Christian faith, say, "Come to Jesus and all your problems will be over." It's just not true. My life didn't begin to be complicated until I became a Christian, because only then did I have to go to war every day between that which is of the flesh and that which is of the Spirit.

The conflict is ongoing because the capacity for evil that resides in the heart of a regenerate person is almost without limit. We ought not to be too shocked when we see Christian leaders falling into serious sin. We have the power of a new life, but that doesn't automatically erase our pre-conversion tendencies (see Gal. 5:16–26; Rom. 6–7). Regeneration is just the beginning. But it's not only just the beginning—it is *the* beginning. It is the most significant beginning that you'll ever have.

We Were Once Dead

I'd like to turn your attention to some very important elements about the beginning of the Christian life. We need to see what we have been regenerated from. At the beginning of the second chapter of his letter to the Ephesians, Paul writes: "And you were dead in the trespasses and sins in which you once walked, following the course of this world" (vv. 1–2a).

We all have values. We all have a perspective, a view of the world and a view of ourselves. We all have preferences. We try to live according to some kind of standard. How do you live your life? What is your standard? Where did you get it? More important, *why* is it your standard?

The apostle declares here, "Before you were reborn, you were dead." Obviously he's not talking about biological death. This message, this letter, is not being sent to a morgue. It is going to people who are biologically alive. Paul is saying that the Ephesians, and we, in the past were dead spiritually. We were spiritual zombies—the walking dead. We were biologically alive but spiritually dead.

How did we walk? Paul says we walked according to "the course of this world." If you run in a marathon with five hundred other contestants, and you decide to go off and run your own course, you are not going to get the prize no matter how fast you run, because you did not stay within the boundaries—within the course—of the race.

There is a definite course that runners are supposed to follow. Paul is saying that before you were regenerate you lived your life according to a course that was set for you by this world.

We humans tend to be slavish in our adherence to the value systems of our peers, particularly in our teen years. Teenagers tend to be very peer conscious. Their constant refrain is, "Everyone is doing it." They seem to lose sleep at night over whether they are up to the minute with the latest fads and fashions. But, of course, at the end of the teenage years we grow out of that, right? You know better than that. We tend to remain conscious of the boundary flags for the course of this world. That slavish adherence to a course that is set out for us by the world is a mark of an unregenerate person, Paul says.

Not only that, Paul says, we lived according to "the prince of the power of the air, the spirit that is now at work in the sons of disobedience—among whom we all once lived in the passions of our flesh, carrying out the desires of the body and the mind, and were by nature children of wrath, like the rest of mankind" (vv. 2b–3).

This is one of the most graphic and detailed descriptions of the moribund, torpid, deadly state of an unregenerate person that we find in all of Scripture. The unregenerate are under the influence of the enemy and seek fulfillment of the lusts of the flesh and the desires of the body and the mind. This is not merely a description of the lifestyles of hardened criminals or convinced hedonists. This is the way everyone lives, without exception. The whole world normally and naturally lives by this fallen course.

But God . . .

All of this description focuses on behavior before the new birth. It's the next word in Ephesians 2 that gets us to regeneration. It's a word that thrills me, for it captures and encapsulates the whole message of redemption: *but*. Paul writes, "But God, who is rich in mercy, for his great love wherewith he loved us, even when we were dead in sins, hath quickened us together with Christ" (vv. 4–5, KJV).

Paul uses a rather obscure word here to refer to the new birth: *quickened*. Biblically speaking, to quicken something is not to make it go faster. It is to make that thing alive. We say in the Apostles' Creed that when Jesus returns He will judge "the quick and the dead." It doesn't say the quick and the slow. The contrast is between those who are alive and those who are dead, and that's the contrast that the apostle is painting here in Ephesians. Once we were dead spiritually, but God quickened us. He made us alive. He brought us out of the state of death. The process by which He did that is regeneration. It is the beginning of the new life.

Furthermore, regeneration is something that is accomplished by God, and only by God. A dead man cannot raise himself from the dead. The only power over death in the universe is the power of God. God alone can bring something out of nothing and life out of death. A dead person can do nothing except stay dead. Our quickening, that first step that brought us into a whole new life and made us new creatures, was accomplished by an act of almighty God.

There are a couple of words that are not part of our everyday Christian jargon, but which are very important for understanding the action of God in regeneration. The words are *monergism* and *synergism*. Let me break these words down for you to help you see what they mean. The prefix *mon* means "one"—something that is single. An *erg* is a unit of labor or of work. We get the word *energy* from this root. So if we put it all together, *monergism* means, literally, "one working." A monergistic work is one in which one party performs the task. The prefix *syn* means "with" or "together with." So a synergistic work is one in which two or more people work together to bring a task to completion. A synergistic work is a cooperative work.

How does this apply to theology and to our discussion of regeneration? Spiritual rebirth is a monergistic work, not a synergistic work. Rebirth is accomplished by God alone. As I mentioned above, a dead man cannot cooperate in his resurrection. Jesus did not go to the tomb of Lazarus and say: "Lazarus, I need you to help Me overcome the dreadful implications of your recent demise." That's not how He talked to Lazarus. Lazarus was helpless and hopeless because he was dead. Bringing a person from spiritual death to spiritual life is something only God can do.

After God makes us alive, then we must become involved. We must believe, repent, and seek after the things of God. But before God makes us alive, we are unable to do these things. We need God to take the initiative to change the disposition of our hearts, quickening our souls so that we can respond by embracing Christ and fleeing to Him in repentance.

The point is that the initiative is from God. Salvation is of the Lord. If you recently have become a Christian, and you're trying to understand what has happened to you, I think it is vitally important that you understand this point early in your Christian development, so that you have the proper appreciation for God's grace established at the very beginning of your walk with Him.

God Accomplishes Regeneration

Some time ago, I was asked to speak to a gathering of men in Jackson, Mississippi. As the day drew near for my visit, the sponsors clued me in that what they wanted from me was not my normal educational speech but an evangelistic message. The message was to be followed by a call to commitment. If ever there was a speaker who was filled with stark, raving terror, it was me when I got this announcement. I have great admiration for those whom God uses as evangelists, but I am a teacher, not an evangelist.

I called them and told them they had the wrong man. I told them that God blesses my teaching, but anytime I try to preach evangelistically, nobody really responds. It's almost like God whispers to me and says, "Hey, that's not your gift." But they wouldn't take no for an answer.

So I preached at the event and I gave a call to commitment. There wasn't a response by the thousands, but to my astonishment, some men committed their lives to Christ for the first time. Later, I sat down with the men who had put the event together and I said: "Do you realize what happened here? While we were engaged in a human gathering, and while I was speaking and reading from the Scriptures, the Creator of the universe came into that room and secretly, invisibly, mysteriously, and supernaturally changed the souls of human beings in there." I told them: "That happened. And God did it."

That night, those men who responded to the gospel, to the extent that they actually possessed the faith they professed, were changed in the depths of their souls. They were redirected from the course of the world to a new course, the course of the Christian life. For those who were spiritually regenerated by the Holy Spirit that night, that meeting was a new beginning. So it is for all who experience the new birth—it is the start of the Christian life.

Chapter Four

Regeneration Is a Sovereign Work of God

Here is a theological formula that may strike you as strange: "Regeneration precedes faith." We have seen that regeneration, or spiritual rebirth, is the beginning of the Christian life. If regeneration is the first step, obviously it must come before the second step. Spiritually dead people do not suddenly develop faith, causing God to regenerate them. Rather, faith is the fruit of the regeneration God performs in our hearts: "Even when we were dead in our trespasses, [God] made us alive together with Christ" (Eph. 2:4b). We are born again (regenerated), then we come to faith, then we are justified, and then we begin to undergo the lifelong sanctification process (Rom. 8:30). All these events comprise the whole complex of the Christian life. But the starting point, the first act in the chain, is all of God—it is a monergistic work, as we saw in the previous chapter.

In short, regeneration is a sovereign work of God. In other words, God exercises His power and His authority over you in His time and His way to bring about the regeneration of your heart. I stress this because many people understand regeneration as merely an activity of moral persuasion whereby God woos or entices us to change and to come in His direction. I am suggesting, following the thinking of Augustine and other giants of the Christian faith, that regeneration is not just God standing apart from us and trying to persuade us to come to Him, but God coming inside of us. He invades the soul, because there has to be a substantive change in the heart before we can come to Christ. In order for us to desire the things of God, we have to be made alive, and to be made alive requires a sovereign act of God.

A Hebrew of Hebrews

In Acts 9, we have the most famous record of a conversion in the history of the church. It is the conversion of Saul, the man who became the apostle Paul. The New Testament teaches that not many wise and great people were called of God to be part of the foundation for the Christian church (1 Cor. 1:26–27). Rather, the early church was made up primarily of the oppressed, the poor, the exploited, and those of limited means. It was part of the plan of God, in the main, to not choose the rich, powerful, and famous for the establishing of His church. But the Scriptures do not say "none" but "not many" were taken from leadership positions or sophisticated levels of status. One who was from such a background was Saul of Tarsus.

Saul was from a family of merchants and had received an extraordinary higher education. Certain experts have maintained that if Saul had never been confronted by Christ on the road to Damascus and radically converted, if God had left him alone to pursue the course he was following, the modern world probably still would be cognizant of him, because he was among the most educated Jews in the first century. He was the star pupil of Gamaliel, the leading rabbi in Jerusalem. He had the equivalent of two PhDs by the time that he was twenty-one years old. As a young man, he had risen in a meteoric fashion to a position of political, theological, and ecclesiastical authority in Israel.

Not only was Saul learned and accomplished, he was highly passionate. He was a zealot. He described himself as "extremely zealous . . . for the traditions of my fathers" (Gal. 1:14b) and as a "Hebrew of Hebrews" (Phil. 3:5). We're not exactly sure what he meant by that, but we know that he was describing himself with a superlative in the Jewish language, similar to the terms "King of kings" or "Lord of lords." In other words, Saul was in a class by himself. He had reached the highest possible level.

Saul was also a Pharisee (Phil. 3:5), a member of the conservative party of Jewish leaders who were committed to strict observance of the Mosaic law. One tradition from the days of the early church suggests that among the Pharisees there was an inner core who held the belief that if any one of them would perfectly keep all the sundry laws they were dedicated to for just one day, that act of virtue would prompt God to send the Messiah. So there was a handful of zealots among the Pharisees who practiced all kinds of self-denial and asceticism. They were devout in their studies and scrupulous to every detail of the law in their attempt to keep it perfectly for a twenty-four-hour period. Some conjecture that Saul himself was one of these zealous Pharisees.

We meet Saul for the first time when he is holding the garments of those who are stoning Stephen (Acts 7:58). In Acts 8 and 9, we see him turn his passion into a militant form of hostility against the nascent church, which he regards as a serious distortion of orthodox Judaism. He sees the Christian movement not as a fulfillment of the Old Testament Scriptures but as the undermining of everything dear to him. So Saul works with the Jewish religious authorities to bring formal charges against the Christians. He is filled with hostility toward Jesus and everything that Jesus stands for.

Christ Confronts Saul

But everything changes in Acts 9, which opens with these words: "But Saul, still breathing threats and murder against the disciples of the Lord, went to the high priest and asked him for letters to the synagogues at Damascus, so that if he found any belonging to the Way, men or women, he might bring them bound to Jerusalem" (vv. 1–2). Every breath

Saul exhaled brought some kind of diabolical threat against the lives of believers, and not just those in Jerusalem. He asked the high priest for letters of official support so he could pursue his investigation, prosecution, and persecution of Christians in Damascus. He wanted to go all the way to Damascus to find any Jews who might have been infected by this Christian heresy. This was akin to a police officer going to a judge to get a court order. Saul wanted to hunt down Christians, both men and women, and bring them in chains to Jerusalem.

But Saul never carried out his mission in Damascus: "Now as he went on his way, he approached Damascus, and suddenly a light from heaven flashed around him. And falling to the ground he heard a voice saying to him, 'Saul, Saul, why are you persecuting me?' And he said, 'Who are you, Lord?' And he said, 'I am Jesus, whom you are persecuting. But rise and enter the city, and you will be told what you are to do'" (vv. 3–6).

If there is any evidence in Scripture that regeneration is a sovereign act, this is it. Saul had done nothing to deserve this marvelous intervention in his life. There was no merit in his work or life that could have induced God to send this gracious visitation; indeed, there was a great deal of demerit. Yet, Jesus came to Saul, and Saul was sovereignly, effectively converted on the spot.

Later, writing as the apostle Paul, he remembered that Jesus also said, "It is hard for you to kick against the goads" (Acts 26:14). That's a strange image. In the ancient world, when oxen were used to pull carts, the oxen sometimes became stubborn, just like mules, and the driver would crack a whip on their backs to get them moving. Sometimes, when the oxen strongly preferred not to move and were displeased by the sting of the whip, they would throw up their back feet and kick, possibly smashing the cart. So people began to put ox goads on the fronts of their carts. On the ox goad, there were strong, sharp spikes that would hurt the oxen's hooves and deter them from kicking. But sometimes an ox that was particularly dumb would "kick against the goads." The pain from kicking against the goad once would make the ox even angrier, and it would kick again even harder. The more it kicked, the more it would hurt, and the more it hurt, the madder it would get, and the madder it got, the more it would kick. The ox would turn itself into a bloody mess as it fought against the ox goad.

Jesus was saying: "Saul, you're a stupid ox. Why are you

persecuting Me? You can't win. You're like an ox kicking against the spikes of an ox goad."

As Saul was lying on the ground, he looked up into the brilliant light and asked, "Who are you, Lord?" He didn't know who had stopped him in his tracks, but he knew that it must be the Lord, for no one else could light up the desert in the middle of the day with a blazing light of reful-gent glory. No one else could knock him to the ground and blind him. No one else could speak to him in a voice from heaven in his own language. It must be the Lord who was speaking to him. Jesus replied: "I am Jesus, whom you are persecuting. But rise and enter the city, and you will be told what you are to do."

Has God Confronted You?

Maybe you have never seen a bright light on the road to Damascus. Maybe you have never been knocked to the ground. I'm confident that you have never heard an audi-ble voice from heaven. In Saul's case, those were simply outward manifestations of the inward, mysterious work of rebirth. But the same sovereign power and authority manifested on the road to Damascus that day has been at work in your soul if indeed you are reborn.

Regeneration is a work of the omnipotent power of God, power that nothing can overcome or resist. If God breathes a person back from the dead, that person comes back from the dead. There is no contest when this power is exercised. God sovereignly confronted Saul and sovereignly changed and redeemed him. Has He done the same for you?

Chapter Five

Regeneration Is Immediate

When I was a child playing outside, my mother would call me in by saying, "R. C., come in for dinner." She would say that a couple of times, but then, if I dawdled too long and tested her patience, she would say, "Young man, get in this house *immediately*," emphasizing every syllable of the word. When I heard that, I knew I needed to get in the house without delay.

In theology, we say that regeneration is immediate. By saying this, we communicate that regeneration is instantaneous; it happens in an instant. But in this case, the meaning of the word *immediate* goes beyond time. To say that regeneration is immediate also means that it occurs without means, without an intervening medium.

Regeneration Is Instantaneous

I noted earlier that I experienced a sudden conversion. Others, however, have very gradual, drawn-out conversion experiences; they may not even know the year in which they became Christians. They say: "I don't know when it happened. It was a gradual thing that occurred over many years." How, then, can I assert that regeneration is instantaneous? The key is in my use of the term *conversion experience*. I'm referring to that of which we are aware. I can say that my awareness of becoming a Christian was sudden, abrupt, and instantaneous. Meanwhile, another person might say, "I just had a gradual awareness." So we can distinguish between our personal consciousness of what God is doing within us and the action itself.

In the 1980s, there was a film titled *Crocodile Dundee* that followed the adventures of a fellow from the Australian

Outback who came to New York City. When he arrived in New York, he was met by a reporter who asked, "How old are you?" He said, "I don't know." She said: "You don't know? How could you not know?" He replied, "Well, I asked the chief of the tribe who knew me when I was born. The chief said, 'In the summer.'" So Crocodile Dundee did not know precisely when he was born. But did that mean he did not have a birthday? No, of course not. There was a time when he was unborn and there was a time when he was born, and the change from one status to the other happened instantaneously (or nearly so). He just didn't know when it happened. In the same manner, there are lots of people that don't know when they were born again.

So a person can be unaware of when or how he became born again. But it is not important to know when or how you became a Christian. The only thing that matters is whether you *are* born again. This is a genuine either/or situation. You're either spiritually dead or you're alive to the things of God. You're either unregenerate or regenerate. There is no in-between state. It's like pregnancy; no one is almost pregnant. Likewise, no one is almost regenerate. You either are or you aren't.

Regeneration Is Without Means

So regeneration is instantaneous. But when I say that regeneration is immediate, I'm saying more than that. I'm saying that when God brings you to spiritual life, He does not use any means apart from Himself to do it. When a doctor treats you for a disease by giving you a prescription, the medicine is the means he uses to bring about your recovery. But the cure for spiritual deadness, regeneration, is not administered in doses. The Great Physician heals immediately.

The Gospel of Mark includes a striking story of a healing Jesus performed. It is an example not of an immediate healing but of a healing that employed means. We read: "And they came to Bethsaida. And some people brought to him a blind man and begged him to touch him" (8:22). Clearly this blind man had friends who cared about him, and since they had heard about the miraculous activity of Jesus, they determined to take their friend to Him. They wanted to see the blind man benefit from Jesus' supernatural power.

Jesus did a strange thing: "And he took the blind man by the hand and led him out of the village" (v. 23a). Picture that. Usually someone would come to Jesus and say, "Jesus,

Son of David, have mercy on me," and when Jesus heard that, He would reply: "I will do so. Go in peace." In other words, Jesus simply healed the person on the spot. But in this case, Jesus took the man away from the crowd so that his healing would not be a public spectacle. Furthermore, Jesus led him *by the hand*. Grace was never more tender than this—God incarnate taking a blind man by the hand and leading him to a private place for healing. What great concern Jesus had for the man's dignity. I wonder how many times that man had been led around by friends. He had had to trust others to guide him. Think of how helpless he was in those situations. But now he was being led by Jesus Christ. He had never had a more trustworthy guide in his life.

Mark then adds: "[He led] him out of the village, and when he had spit on his eyes and laid his hands on him, he asked him, 'Do you see anything?'" (v. 23b). I have just labored the point that Jesus bent over backward to protect this blind man's dignity. Yet as soon as He got him away from the watching crowd, He spat in his eyes. In our culture, that would be a gesture of insult designed to humiliate. But obviously that was not the intent of Jesus. When Jesus spat in the eyes of the blind man and laid His

51

hands on him, He was communicating with the man via touch.

This story is similar to an account in John 9, which also speaks of Jesus healing a blind man using saliva. On that occasion, however, He didn't spit in the man's eyes; rather, He mixed spittle with dirt to form mud, then put some of the mud on the man's eyes in order to heal him.

What was going on in these incidents? Was Jesus using home remedies for curing blindness that His mother taught Him back in Nazareth? No, there was no special therapeutic power in the spit or the mud. I have no idea why Jesus used these methods, but given the countless healings Jesus performed without such means, I know that He did not need to use spit or mud to give these men their sight. The power to impart vision was not in the spit or in the mud. In other words, the power was not in the means—even though Jesus used means in both cases. The efficacy was in the power of God that lay behind the means.

What happened was strange. Jesus spat in the blind man's eyes, laid His hands on him, and asked him, "Do you see anything?" The man opened his eyes and said, "I see men, but they look like trees, walking" (Mark 8:24).

This is a marked improvement—the man could not see

anything walking prior to this encounter with Christ. This man had been totally blind. Now at least he saw vague, shadowy forms in motion. Shouldn't the man have been satisfied with this?

I've never seen men who look like trees, but I've seen trees that look like men. There was a large oak tree behind Wiegel's grocery store when I was growing up, and every night after dark, in the moonlight, I had to take the path through the woods behind the store to get to my home on McClellan Drive. Every night I would look up and see the silhouette of this massive tree, which looked as if it had a hundred hostile arms reaching out to grab me. I used to run past that tree because it looked like a man—a particularly grotesque and threatening man. But I've never seen a man who looked like a tree.

A Second Touch

What happened next? "Then Jesus laid his hands on his eyes again; and he opened his eyes, his sight was restored, and he saw everything clearly" (v. 25). With this second touch from Jesus, the man's vision was fully restored.

The point of this story is not to teach us about

regeneration. The point is simply to record for us a historical incident that displayed the power of Christ in healing a man who was suffering from blindness. But I think there are some principles we can draw here. I think there is a legitimate analogy to the Christian life that can be drawn from this account.

In the first place, regeneration is not gradual. It doesn't take two touches of Christ to change a man's heart from stone to flesh. It doesn't take two touches of the finger of God to bring life out of death. It takes only one.

But have you noticed that when we are reborn, when we are spiritually awakened, we are not instantaneously cured of all sin? Again, rebirth is a beginning, but we still carry around with us that body of death that fights and kicks against the life that the Spirit of God has made within us. Spiritually, when we are born again, the best we can hope for initially is to see men like trees walking.

Back when the "I Found It" bumper-sticker fad was at its peak, I reacted with a bit of annoyance whenever I saw one. I understood what that slogan meant—people were saying they had found the pearl of great price, the most precious commodity in this universe. However, when the New Testament talks about seeking after God and the kingdom of God, it is referring to Christians. The quest for God, seeking after Him, starts at rebirth. When a prospector finds a nugget of gold, does he stop looking? No, he starts looking with greater vigor than ever, and he looks in the same area where he found the first one, because he figures where there's one nugget there must be more. In just the same way, when we experience new life, we want more new life. We want to grow. We want to come to the fullness of maturity.

The blind man must have been thrilled to see men who looked like trees walking around. But I can see him, with lips quivering, saying, "Jesus, as long as you're here, would you give me one more touch, because I'd like to see it all?" So Jesus touched him again, and everything came into focus. Now he could see men as men walking and trees as trees swaying in the breeze. Now he could distinguish between a man and a tree, because he saw clearly.

Growth in Grace Is Mediated

The New Testament often uses blindness as a metaphor for spiritual deadness. By analogy, regeneration is something like being given sight. We are shrouded in darkness, but the light breaks into our lives and we suddenly see the sweetness of the things of God and delight in those things that are hidden from other people who don't recognize their beauty. Do you have friends who just can't understand why you're so excited about your faith? They just can't see it. They can't understand it. They don't perceive what you're talking about.

But even we don't see it perfectly. We need to have our vision increased. When we are born again, without means, by the sovereign power of God, that is just the beginning. We then begin the life of spiritual growth.

In order to see more clearly, what must we do? I cannot call on Jesus to come and touch my eye again—or, more properly, my heart or my soul. Yes, He is present through His Spirit, but the growth by which we are to come to maturity happens by means that we must use. That is, spiritual growth is not immediate but is mediated. Spiritual growth requires making use of what we call the means of grace—the Bible, prayer, fellowship, and church involvement.

Do you want to grow? Do you want your vision to be sharper? Then you must be diligent and disciplined in the study of the Scriptures. By studying the content of this book, your vision and understanding will be clarified. If you are going to grow closer to God, you have to communicate with Him, and that requires spending time in prayer. If you want to grow in sanctification, you need to spend time with Christians who are more mature than you are and benefit from the fellowship of their company. If you want to grow into maturity as a Christian, you must become involved in your church. Church membership is not an option for the Christian. Christ established His church and commands His people to be a part of it, because participation in the church (attendance, membership, service, worship) is a means of grace. It is a means by which your new life is nurtured so that you can grow.

We Work and God Works

In short, if you want to get past the confusion that is still a part of your young Christian life, you must work at it. We have seen that regeneration is monergistic, a work of God alone. But growth in the Christian life is synergistic—we work toward it along with God. What does the New Testament say? "Work out your own salvation with fear and trembling" (Phil. 2:12b). This is a call to labor.

There are several parts of the package of salvation. It starts with regeneration (which is instantaneous), but there is an outworking that has to take place, and that outworking is to be done through the application of all of the effort that we can bring to it. We can't simply go to sleep and say: "God sovereignly knocked me off my horse on the road to Damascus. He started it; let Him finish it. I'm going to let Him do it all." No, we're called to work out our salvation fearfully, not in the sense of intimidation but in the sense of careful diligence.

As we work, we know this: "It is God who works in you, both to will and to work for his good pleasure" (Phil. 2:13). We are to work just as God works. In this manner, that which God has begun in you will be brought to finality. Jesus Christ, who took you by the hand, led you away, spat in your eye, and gave you sight to see things previously concealed from you, will touch you again and again so that your understanding of the things of God will grow clearer and sharper. But you must work with Him. Your Christian maturity will reach a level that is in direct proportion to your willingness to labor in this great vocation.

Chapter Six

Regeneration Is Permanent

When God brings about our spiritual rebirth, He does not let anything extinguish that life. Rather, those whom He makes alive He preserves and keeps alive, that they might one day reach the goal for which He regenerated them. This is why Paul tells us that "he who began a good work in you will bring it to completion at the day of Jesus Christ" (Phil. 1:6).

In our exploration of the doctrine of regeneration, or spiritual rebirth, we have seen so far that regeneration is necessary, that it is mysterious, that it is only a beginning, that it is sovereign, and that it is immediate. In this chapter, I want to explore an aspect of regeneration that we often fail to consider, an aspect that is a point of confusion for many. It is the truth that regeneration is permanent. If it were up to us, we would find every possible way to lose our regeneration. But God will not allow that to happen; He will bring us to the fullness of our redemption.

"Who Do You Say That I Am?"

The person in the New Testament who perhaps best symbolizes the permanence of regeneration is the apostle Peter. But Peter was not always called Peter; he was Simon Bar-Jonah until Jesus renamed him. What was the occasion for the bestowal of this new name?

During the earthly ministry of Jesus, the disciples spent a considerable amount of time with Him. They were able to watch His activities. They saw Him heal the sick (Luke 8:40–48). They saw Him calm the tempest (Luke 7:22–25). They saw Him walk on water (Matt. 14:22–32). They saw Him turn water into wine (John 2:1–12). They saw Him raise people from the dead (Luke 7:11–17). They listened to His teaching (Matt. 5–7). In short, they had the opportunity to see Jesus with a degree of intimacy that the multitudes did not enjoy.

On a particular occasion in Caesarea Philippi, Jesus withdrew from the multitudes and spent time with His inner core of friends and disciples (Matt. 16:13–20). During that time, Jesus said to them: "Who do people say that I am? What's the scuttlebutt out there? Have they caught on yet? What's public opinion about My ministry right now?" One by one, His disciples gave answers to the question: "Well, Jesus, some say You're Elijah, some say You're John the Baptist, and some say that You're a prophet." Jesus said: "That's interesting. But you have an intimate view of who I am and what I've been doing. What's your opinion? Who do you say that I am? What do you think?" Simon acted as the spokesman for the twelve and responded to the question with this affirmation: "You are the Christ, the Son of the living God" (v. 16).

This was a profound and bold statement from the mouth of a Jew. A first-century Jew who had been watching Jesus looked at Him and said, "You're the Messiah." Our

English word *Christ* comes from the Greek word *Christos*, which translates the Hebrew *mashiyach* ("messiah"). Peter was effectively saying: "You are the One for whom we Jews have been dreaming, praying, and hoping for centuries. You are the One who was promised to Abraham, to David, to Jeremiah. You are the Christ, the Son of the living God."

Peter the Rock

When Jesus heard that statement from Simon, He pronounced a benediction. He looked at His disciple and said: "Blessed are you, Simon Bar-Jonah! For flesh and blood has not revealed this to you, but my Father who is in heaven" (v. 17). In other words: "Simon, you didn't come to this conclusion through your own unaided intellectual ability. To see what you see, to understand what you understand, requires divine assistance. God has unveiled a mystery to you. He has made clear to you what other people are missing every day. You are blessed that you see what you see."

It is crucial that we never forget that we have been given the new birth by the Spirit of God. We should never forget who has done this thing for us and how blessed we are to have experienced the second birth, this touch from the hand of God. Like Peter, we have received God's healing touch so that we see what others do not see.

Then Jesus turned to His disciple and said, "And I tell you, you are Peter, and on this rock I will build my church" (v. 18a). There has been a great deal of debate about what Jesus meant by that statement. Some believe Jesus was saying He was going to build His church on Peter himself, and therefore this particular disciple came to have primacy in the Roman Catholic Church. Others look at this statement as an indication that Jesus was going to build His church on this confession of faith, so that anyone who professes that Jesus is the Christ is incorporated into His church. In other words, a person must open his or her mouth and say, "You are the Christ." It is as if Jesus was saying: "You're the rock, Peter, the one who has made this first confession, and this is where we will start. We're going to start to build right now, right here. From this point, I will build My church."

Sifted Like Wheat

Of course, as we see later in the Gospel records, Peter did not always behave like a rock. It's a wonder Jesus did not say, "You are a loaf of bread that crumbles into pieces," or "You are a piece of cake," or "You are a marshmallow." Yes, Peter had moments when he stood firm, but at a time of testing, he failed miserably.

According to Luke's account of the night of Jesus' betrayal, as He was enjoying His final celebration of the Passover, which also was the first celebration of the Lord's Supper, He said, "You are those who have stayed with me in my trials, and I assign to you, as my Father assigned to me, a kingdom, that you may eat and drink at my table in my kingdom and sit on thrones judging the twelve tribes of Israel" (Luke 22:28–30). Jesus said to His friends: "You have been loyal to Me and I'm going to be loyal to you. I'm going to see to it that you will sit on thrones of judgment."

But then Jesus turned to Peter and said: "Simon, Simon, behold, Satan demanded to have you, that he might sift you like wheat. But I have prayed for you that your faith may not fail. And when you have turned again, strengthen your brothers" (vv. 31–32). What was He saying here? "Simon, you think you're a rock. But Satan wants you. He wants to sift you. He wants to turn you into putty in his hands. He wants to play with you. He wants to use you as a vehicle to get at Me. I just said that everyone here has been loyal and faithful to me, but you, Simon, are going to betray me." However, along with the bad news, Jesus offered Peter this wonderful assurance: "But I have prayed for you that your faith may not fail."

How did Peter respond to this stunning warning? He said, "Lord, I am ready to go with you both to prison and to death" (v. 33). When I first became a Christian, a group of men at my college gathered every Wednesday night for a Bible study and for the singing of hymns around the piano. I learned many Christian hymns for the first time on those nights, and one of those hymns was "Where He Leads Me." I can remember singing those words with all the gusto of a new convert: "Where He leads me I will follow; I'll go with Him, with Him, all the way." When I hear that song now, I feel guilty, because I want to be careful before I say I'll do anything or go anywhere. In our youthful exuberance, we make all kinds of boasts about our commitment and our loyalty that only time and endurance can verify. Sadly, as the years of our pilgrimage pass, we learn just how prone we are to failure.

Peter was like me in my youthful exuberance. He was saying: "Jesus, You are the Christ, the Son of the living God. Where You lead me, I will follow. I will go to prison with You if I have to. I'll even follow You to the death." He had not yet learned how vulnerable he was.

The Denial and the Betrayal

Peter made his bold claim of loyalty in the upper room on Thursday evening, the night before Good Friday. Where was Peter later that night? As soon as the soldiers came to arrest Jesus, Peter fled. He lurked outside the high priest's house while the Jewish officials were inside judging Jesus, trying to get some report of what was going on and to learn the fate of his Master. Then a maid—not the sergeant at arms, not the captain of the guard—came over and said, "You also were with Jesus the Galilean" (Matt. 26:69), but Peter denied it. Later, another maid said, "This man was with Jesus of Nazareth" (v. 71), but Peter denied it with an oath. Finally, a bystander said, "Certainly you too are one of them, for your accent betrays you" (v. 73). Did Peter say, "No"? Not exactly. The Bible says he denied it with curses.

He started swearing like a sailor, emphasizing that he did not know Jesus—all because he was terrified by these maids and bystanders. What happened? "The Rock" was sifted like wheat. The moment of testing came, and Peter failed.

Earlier that night, at the Lord's Supper, Jesus had said, "Truly I say to you, one of you will betray me" (Matt. 26:21). The disciples around the table, looking at Jesus apprehensively, said, one after another, "Is it I, Lord?" (v. 22). Then they came to the treasurer. Judas said, "Is it I, Rabbi?" Jesus said, "You have said so" (v. 25). John adds that Jesus said, "What you are going to do, do quickly," and Judas then went out into the night (John 13:27, 30).

Thus, Jesus dismissed Judas to his treachery. The Scriptures say that Judas already had agreed to give Jesus into the hands of His enemies in exchange for thirty pieces of silver (Matt. 26:14–16; Mark 14:10–11; Luke 22:3–6). When that deed was done, Judas hanged himself. He died in total disgrace, without his thirty pieces of silver, and with the legacy that has made his name a symbol of treachery and betrayal for all of human history.

What was the difference between these two men? The answer appears in Jesus' High Priestly Prayer: "While I was with them, I kept them in your name, which you have given me. I have guarded them, and not one of them has been lost except the son of destruction, that the Scripture might be fulfilled" (John 17:12). Simply put, Judas was never regenerate, but Peter was a regenerate son of God, and therefore the power of God kept him. Peter's regeneration was permanent. Even though Peter fell violently, dramatically, and abysmally, his fall was neither total nor final.

Peter was preserved by the One who had quickened him in the first place. The Holy Spirit not only is the causal agent for regeneration, but according to the Scriptures, He is "the earnest of our inheritance" (Eph. 1:14, KJV). We sometimes speak of "earnest money," which is something like a down payment. In a real estate transaction, the party making the purchase puts down some earnest money, which shows he is a serious buyer who intends to complete the transaction. Likewise, when God regenerates someone through the Spirit, He gives the Spirit to be with that person permanently. The presence of the Spirit is an "earnest" that God eventually will give that person all that goes with regeneration. Though human beings fail to complete their transactions from time to time, despite earnest money, God always does what He says He will do.

He finishes the contract. He completes the deal. He never defaults. He never misses a payment. When God the Holy Spirit quickens you, you can be sure that your salvation is permanent.

Celebrate the New Birth

So we celebrate what it means to be born again. There is no greater gift a human being can receive. There is no more important treasure that a human being can possess. If you cannot say for certain that you are born of the Spirit, I plead with you to recall the teaching of Jesus that unless a person is born of the Spirit he cannot see the kingdom of God or enter it (John 3:3, 5). Unless you are born again, you will miss the kingdom of God. But if you are born again, you will know the sweetness and the mercy of God. You will know the power of a new life. You will be a new creature, a new creation that nothing can destroy. Neither life nor death nor things present nor things past nor powers nor principalities nor heights nor depths nor any other thing will be able to separate you from the love that is in Christ (Rom. 8:38–39).

About the Author

Dr. R.C. Sproul was founder of Ligonier Ministries, founding pastor of Saint Andrew's Chapel in Sanford, Fla., first president of Reformation Bible College, and executive editor of *Tabletalk* magazine. His radio program, *Renewing Your Mind*, is still broadcast daily on hundreds of radio stations around the world and can also be heard online. He was author of more than one hundred books, including *The Holiness of God, Chosen by God,* and *Everyone's a Theologian*. He was recognized throughout the world for his articulate defense of the inerrancy of Scripture and the need for God's people to stand with conviction upon His Word.

Free eBooks *by*
R.C. Sproul

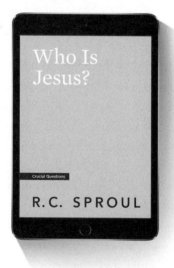

Does prayer really change things? Can I be sure I'm saved? Dr. R.C. Sproul answers these important questions, along with more than twenty-five others, in his Crucial Questions series. Designed for the Christian or thoughtful inquirer, these booklets can be used for personal study, small groups, and conversations with family and friends. Browse the collection and download your free digital ebooks today.

Get 3 free months
of *Tabletalk*

In 1977, R.C. Sproul started *Tabletalk* magazine.
Today it has become the most widely read subscriber-based monthly
devotional magazine in the world. **Try it free for 3 months.**

ASK LIGONIER

Do we have free will?

Why did God kill Uzzah?

Is it true that God controls everything?

A Place to Find Answers

Maybe you're leading a Bible study tomorrow. Maybe you're just beginning to dig deeper. It's good to know that you can always ask Ligonier. For more than forty-five years, Christians have been looking to Ligonier Ministries, the teaching fellowship of R.C. Sproul, for clear and helpful answers to biblical and theological questions. Now you can ask those questions as they arise, confident that our team will work quickly to provide clear, concise, and trustworthy answers. When you have questions, just ask Ligonier.

FOR MORE INFORMATION, VISIT LIGONIER.ORG/ASK